ME AN MACHINES

SPORTS CARS

CHRIS OXLADE

Raintree

Chicago, Illinois

For information, address the publisher:
Raintree, 100 N. LaSalle, Suite 1200
Chicago, IL 60602
Customer Service: 888-363-4266
Visit our website at www.raintreelibrary.com

Printed and bound in China by South China Printing Company
09 08 07 06 05
10 9 8 7 6 5 4 3 2 1

Library of Congress Cataloging-in-Publication Data
Oxlade, Chris.
  Sports cars / Christopher Oxlade.
    p. cm. -- (Mean machines)
  Includes bibliographical references and index.
  ISBN 1-4109-1084-9 (library binding - hardcover) -- ISBN 1-4109-1199-3
(pbk.) 1. Sports cars--Juvenile literature. I. Title. II. Series.
  TL236.O95 2004
  629.222'1--dc22
                          2004015341

Acknowledgments
The publishers would like to thank the following for permission to reproduce photographs:
Alvey & Towers Picture Library: p. 31; Aston Martin: title page, pp. 5, 35 (t); BMW: pp. 11 (t), 23; Bob Masters Photography: p. 32 (t); Bugatti: p. 57 (b); Chrysler: pp. 5 (t,r), 8 (b), 9 (b), 16, 21, 27 (t), 43 (t), 57 (t); Corbis: pp. 6 (b) (Richard Olivier), 9 (t) (Andrew DeMattos), 10 (t) (Pitchal FR), 13 (b) (Alain Denize), 14 (World Racing Images), 24 (l) (George D. Lepp), 28 (Vittoriano Rastelli), 34 (Ben Wood), 35 (b) (Joseph Sohm/ChromoSohm Inc.), 36 (Kim Sayer), 40 (l) (Cy Jariz Cyrl/NewSport), 41 (t) (Alan Schein Photography), 45 (b) (Jean-Francois Galeron/World Racing Images), 48 (Joseph Sohm/ChromoSohm Inc.), 49 (t) (Hulton-Deutsch Collection), 49 (b) (Robert Dowling), 50 (David Lees), 51 (t) (George D. Lepp), 52 (t) (Bettmann), 52 (b) (Ted Soqui), 53 (t) (Joseph Sohm/ChromoSohm Inc.), 53 (b) (Ted Soqui), 54 (t) (Bettmann), 56 (Ted Soqui); Corbis Sygma: pp. 46 (t) (Bembaron Jeremy), 51 (b) (Nogues Alain); Ford: p. 6 (t); Honda: pp. 12–13 (t); Mazda: pp. 8 (l), 10, 11, 26; Mercedes: pp. 29, 39 (t); Morgan Motor Company: p. 37 (b); Neill Bruce: pp. 25 (t), 30, 32 (b), 33, 37 (t); Noble Automotive Limited: pp. 18 (b), 19 (b); Peugeot Sport UK: pp. 17 (r), 26 (t), 38, 39 (b), 44, 45 (t), 46 (b), 47; Porsche: pp. 4, 5 (m,r), 16, 17, 22, 42, 43 (b), 54 (b), 55; Tim Skipper/www.sports190.com: p. 15; TVR: pp. 19 (t), 24 (b), 25 (b).

Cover photograph of a Ferrari F1 convertible reproduced with permission of Alvey & Towers Picture Library.

Every effort has been made to contact copyright holders of any material reproduced in this book.
Any omissions will be rectified in subsequent printings if notice is given to the publishers.

The paper used to print this book comes from sustainable resources.

CONTENTS

Any words appearing in the text in bold, **like this,** are explained in the glossary. You can also look out for them in the "Up to Speed" box at the bottom of each page.

FAST AND FURIOUS

SPORTS CAR TERMS

Some sidebars in this book contain technical details about sports cars. This is what some of the words in these sidebars mean:

hp: Short for **horsepower.** Engine power is measured in hp.

mph: Short for miles per hour.

km/h: Short for kilometers per hour.

rpm: Short for **revolutions** per minute.

The driver turns a key and puts the car into **gear.** He presses his foot onto the **accelerator** and the engine roars to life. The tires screech on the **tarmac** and the car leaps forward. The driver is thrown back into the seat as the car speeds away. Seconds later, the car is moving along at terrifying speeds. This is no ordinary car! It is a sports car. It is **sleek** and powerful. It was built for having fun!

FAMOUS NAMES

There are plenty of famous sports car makers and plenty of famous sports cars. Have you heard of Ferrari, Jaguar, Lamborghini, and Audi? They are all sports car makers. What about the *Viper,* the *Corvette,* the *Testarossa,* and the *DB9?* These are all famous sports cars.

accelerator   foot pedal used to make a car's engine produce more or less power

ASTON MARTIN DB9

- Date production started: 2003
- **Chassis** (pronounced "chass-ee"), the structure of a car: **aluminum** frame
- Engine position: front (see pages 14–15)
- Engine type: 6.0-liter V12 (see pages 22–23)
- Power: 450 hp
- **Acceleration**: 0–60 mph (96 km/h) in 4.7 seconds
- Top speed: 186 mph (298 km/h)

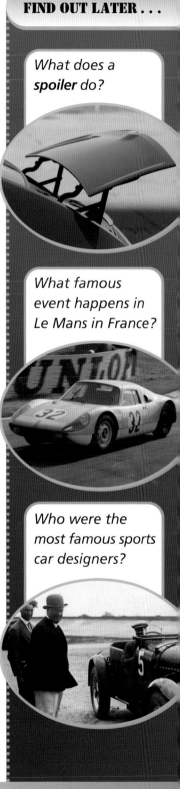

*What does a **spoiler** do?*

What famous event happens in Le Mans in France?

Who were the most famous sports car designers?

ROAD AND TRACK

You often see beautiful sports cars whizzing by on the streets. This is where most owners drive their cars. But to see sports cars performing at their best, you have to go to a race track. Here, you can watch expert racing drivers thundering around corners at incredible speeds.

aluminum   strong, lightweight metal
tarmac   hard, smooth road covering

ON THE ROAD

What is a sports car? There's no exact answer to this question. But it is different from an ordinary family car. A sports car is normally rather small. It is lower to the ground than a normal car. The biggest difference between a sports car and a family car is **performance.** Performance is how quickly a car can accelerate and how fast it can go. Sports cars have great **performance.** A sports car must also **handle** well. That means it must go around corners at high speed without spinning out of control.

PERFORMANCE FIGURES

Sports car **enthusiasts** like to compare the performances of different cars. Performance is measured by **acceleration** and top speed. Acceleration can be measured by the time it takes the car to reach 60 mph (96 km/h) from standing still.

The 165-mph (265-km/h) Dodge *Viper* is one of the best American sports cars.

UP TO SPEED   accelerate   speed up
chassis   framework that supports a car's body

FUN TO DRIVE

People can drive sports cars on public roads. However, there are speed limits for safety on public roads, so sports car owners cannot drive their machines at top speeds. They have to go to a race track instead.

People still love driving sports cars on the roads within the legal speed limit. They enjoy feeling the power from the engine as the car accelerates. They love the rush of the wind while driving in a **convertible.**

BMW Z8

- Date production started: 2000
- Where made: Germany
- **Chassis**: tubular **aluminum**
- Engine position: front (see pages 14–15)
- Engine type: 5.0-liter V8 (see pages 22–23)
- Power: 394 **hp**
- Acceleration: 0–60 mph (96 km/h) in 4.7 seconds
- Top speed: 155 mph (249 km/h)

enthusiast person who really enjoys a particular hobby
performance measure of a car's acceleration and top speed

SPORTY LOOKS

There are lots of differences between a sports car and an ordinary four-seater family car. The difference that is easiest to see is the shape. A sports car has a smoother, lower body than a family car. This smooth shape lets the car move easily through the air. A sports car is low to the ground to keep its center of gravity low. Its center of gravity is the point around which it balances. A low center of gravity makes a sports car very stable. It lets the car go around corners fast without tipping over.

TWO SEATS

Most sports cars have only two seats, one for the driver and one for a passenger. Sometimes there is a small, cramped space for another passenger behind. There's not much room for luggage.

TECH TALK

Features of a sports car
- Smooth body
- Low, wide shape
- Lightweight parts
- Powerful engine

LIGHT AND POWERFUL

Sports cars can pull away quickly from a standing start. They speed up quickly, too. We say that sports cars have good **acceleration.** Acceleration depends on weight and power. The lighter the car and the more powerful its engine, the better its acceleration will be. Sports cars are lightweight and have powerful engines. A powerful engine also gives the car a good top speed.

TWO DOORS

Most sports cars have two doors, one on each side. A few have no doors at all—the driver has to climb into the top. Some sports cars feature doors called scissor doors. They open upward instead of outward.

This front view of a Dodge *Viper* shows its low, **sleek** shape.

sleek   smooth, with graceful lines

RENAULT CLIO SPORT

- Date production started: 1998
- Where made: France
- **Chassis: unitary**
- Engine position: front (see pages 14–15)
- Engine type: 3.0-liter V6 (see pages 22–23)
- Power: 230 **hp**
- **Acceleration:** 0–60 mph (96 km/h) in 6.7 seconds
- Top speed: 145 mph (233 km/h)

SPORTS CAR STYLES

All sports cars are **sleek,** low machines. But that's only half the story. They come in different styles, and each style has its own name. A **roadster** is a two-seater sports car with no roof. There is just a windshield to protect the passengers from the wind and rain. This style of car is sometimes called a spyder. This was the Italian name given to a roadster in the early 1900s. A **coupe** (pronounced "koop") is a sports car with a body that curves gently from the roof to the rear. This style of car is often known as a **grand tourer,** or GT.

alloy wheels　wheels made from lightweight alloy metal
convertible　car with a roof that can be removed

CONVERTIBLES

Many sports cars are also **convertibles.** A convertible has a roof that the driver can put on when it is cold or rainy or take off when it is dry and sunny. Convertibles have either soft tops or hard tops. Soft tops are made of fabric on a metal frame. Hard tops are made of metal or plastic. Tops can be removed completely or can fold down into a space in the trunk. Cars with folding roofs are often called **drop-tops.**

MODIFICATIONS

A few sports cars are sporty versions of ordinary cars with four seats, a fixed roof, and luggage space in the trunk. These sports cars have more powerful engines than ordinary cars and other unique features such as **spoilers** and **alloy wheels.**

The Mazda *RX-8* is a coupe.

unitary chassis framework that includes a car's side and roof panels, floor, and engine compartment

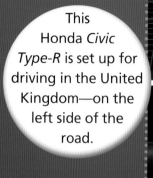

This Honda *Civic Type-R* is set up for driving in the United Kingdom—on the left side of the road.

REV COUNTER RED LINE

The speed of an engine is measured in **revolutions** per minute (rpm). A red line on the rev counter shows the driver the maximum speed that the engine can turn without being damaged.

SPORTY INTERIORS

The outside of a sports car is different from the outside of an ordinary family car. But how is the inside of a sports car different? How do the dashboard, seats, and controls look? Some very expensive sports cars offer many **luxuries.** They use expensive materials such as leather and polished wood. Other sports cars are very simple inside. This is to keep the car's weight down for maximum **performance.** Even some incredibly expensive cars have very simple interiors.

crankshaft   part of an engine that turns and is connected to the transmission

Most sports cars have manual **transmission.** That means the driver changes **gears** to go faster or slower by moving a stick shift. A few sports cars have semiautomatic transmissions. The driver changes gears by pulling on small paddles on the steering wheel.

INSTRUMENTS

A sports car needs the same instruments as any other car. But the most important are the **speedometer** and **rev counter.** The speedometer shows the car's speed, and the rev counter shows how quickly the engine's **crankshaft** is turning.

SEATS AND BELTS

As a sports car **accelerates,** brakes, and speeds around corners, the driver and passenger are thrown around. Sports car seats have side supports to stop people from sliding backward, forward, or sideways. They are called bucket seats. Sports cars often have four-point seat belts, which hold people in their seats more firmly than normal three-point belts.

revolution   one complete turn
transmission   machinery that connects a car's engine to its wheels

ENGINE POSITIONS

The engine of a sports car gives it its speedy **performance.** Together with the **transmission,** the engine makes up the heaviest part of a car. The position of this weight in the car is important for good **handling.**

FRONT AND REAR

In most ordinary cars, the engine is at the front. It is ahead of the driver. This means that most of the weight of the engine is on the front wheels. Most sports cars also have engines in front. Front-engined sports cars often have a long **hood.** A few sports cars have the engine behind the rear wheels. The back of a rear-engined car tends to swing out on corners if the driver is not very careful. This puts the car into a spin.

DRIVING WHEELS

The driving wheels are the wheels that the engine turns around. Sports cars either have **rear-wheel drive, front-wheel drive,** or **four-wheel drive.** Most sports cars have rear-wheel drive. This helps to stop the wheels from spinning, because the car leans back onto the rear wheels as the car accelerates, pressing them onto the road. This Citroën is a four-wheel drive **rally** car.

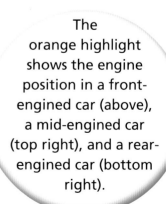

The orange highlight shows the engine position in a front-engined car (above), a mid-engined car (top right), and a rear-engined car (bottom right).

front-wheel drive   vehicle with front wheels turned directly by the engine

MID-ENGINES

Some sports cars have mid-engines. That means that the engine is behind the driver but in front of the rear wheels. It is where the back seats would be in a normal family car. The weight of the engine is shared between the front and back wheels. A mid-engined car turns into corners better than a front-engined car.

PAGANI ZONDA

- Date production started: 1999
- Where made: Italy
- **Chassis: monocoque**
- Engine position: mid-engined
- Engine type: 6.0-liter V12 (see pages 22–23)
- Power: 388 **hp**
- **Acceleration:** 0–60 mph (96 km/h) in 4.5 seconds
- Top speed: 200 mph (322 km/h)

monocoque   single-piece chassis
rear-wheel drive   vehicle with rear wheels turned directly by the engine

SPORTS CAR PARTS

Sports cars must have quick **acceleration**, reach top speeds, and have stable **handling.** This is not easy for **manufacturers** to achieve. They use special car bodies, special engines, and many other special parts for their cars. You can't build a sports car from ordinary car parts!

SMOOTH BODIES

Sports car bodies are not made in **sleek** shapes just to look good. A smooth, curved shape is important for **performance**, too. It is all related to **aerodynamics.**

SPOILERS AND WINGS

Sports cars often have a piece like a shelf at the rear. This is called a **spoiler.** It reduces drag. Some sports cars have a wing instead of a spoiler. At high speed, it presses the car's wheels onto the road for better grip.

Air flowing smoothly over a sports-car body in a wind tunnel.

aerodynamics   science of how air flows around moving objects

PUSHING THE AIR ASIDE

As a car speeds along, it must push the air in front of it aside. The air causes a force on the front of the car that tries to slow the car down. The force is called air resistance, or **drag.** The faster a car goes, the bigger the drag gets. Eventually, drag stops a car from going any faster. Air flows more easily around a smooth car than around a vehicle with a bulky shape. The smooth car has less drag on it, so it can go faster.

REDUCING DRAG

Any part of a car that sticks out into the air creates drag. The only bits that stick out from a very fast sports car are the wing mirrors. These are specially designed to make as little drag as possible. To avoid drag, sports cars have pop-up headlights or headlights built into the shape of the car.

The bottom of a sports car is very close to the ground. This helps to reduce drag and sucks the car down onto the road. The front air **deflector** pushes air into the engine **cooling ducts** and around the car's sides.

cooling ducts   one of the pipes that carries air to an engine to cool it
drag   force that tries to stop things from moving through the air

17

SPORTS CHASSIS

The main part of a car is its **chassis.** All the other parts of a car attach to the chassis. A chassis must be strong for safety and for **handling.** Ordinary family cars have a one-piece chassis made from steel. It includes side and roof panels, a floor, and an engine compartment. This is called a **unitary chassis.**

Steel is a heavy material. For good **acceleration** and braking, a sports car needs to be lightweight. A steel unitary chassis would slow its **performance.** Sports cars are made lightweight by using special materials and structures.

SPECIAL MATERIALS

Many sports cars have a unitary body shell made from **aluminum.** Doors and **hoods** are made from aluminum, too. Aluminum is lighter than steel, but it is more expensive. Body panels are often made from other tough lightweight materials, such as plastic, **carbon fiber,** and **kevlar.**

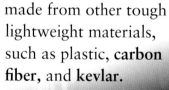

carbon fiber   very hard, strong, light material
hood   movable metal cover over the front of a car

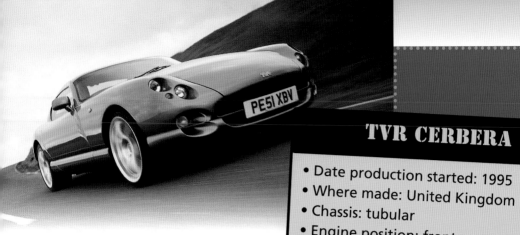

TVR CERBERA

- Date production started: 1995
- Where made: United Kingdom
- Chassis: tubular
- Engine position: front
- Engine type: 4.2-liter V8 (see pages 22–23)
- Power: 350 **hp**
- Acceleration: 0–60 mph (96 km/h) in 4.0 seconds
- Top speed: 185 mph (297 km/h)

INTERNAL FRAMES

Very light, very fast sports cars do not normally have unitary bodies. Instead, they have a lightweight internal frame. Thin body panels are attached to it. The frame gives the car strength and supports the engine and other parts. The body panels give it style and make it **aerodynamic.** Some sports cars have a space frame. This is made from steel or aluminum tubes, a little like a bicycle frame.

The Noble *M12* is built around a steel space-frame chassis.

POWERFUL ENGINES

A sports car engine is very similar to the engine of a normal family car. It is called an **internal combustion** engine and looks like a big block of metal. Inside are spaces called **cylinders.** They are the shape of tin cans. Inside each cylinder is a **piston.** The piston fits tightly into the cylinder, but it can slide in and out. The engine's power comes from tiny explosions that push the pistons outward. The moving pistons make a part called a **crankshaft** turn. The crankshaft drives the car's wheels, and the car speeds off.

INSIDE AN ENGINE

Four strokes
These are the strokes of a four-stroke engine.

1. Intake stroke
Piston moves out of the cylinder. Air and fuel mixture goes into the cylinder.

2. Compression stroke
Piston moves into the cylinder. Air and fuel is crushed into the top of the cylinder.

3. Power stroke
Fuel and air explodes. Piston is pushed out of the cylinder.

4. Exhaust stroke
Piston moves into the cylinder. Waste gases are pushed out of the cylinder.

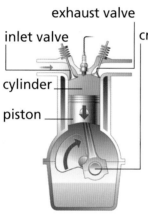

exhaust valve
inlet valve
crankshaft
cylinder
piston

1. Intake stroke

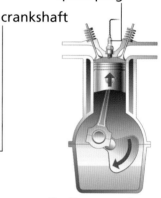

spark plug

2. Compression stroke

3. Power stroke

4. Exhaust stroke

internal combustion what happens when fuel burns inside an engine

FOUR-STROKE CYCLE

The pistons in an engine keep going out then in, out then in. Each movement in or out is called a stroke. Every piston does a pattern of four strokes. Each pattern is called a cycle. During each cycle, fuel is burned in the cylinder to make an explosion. **Exhaust** made by the explosion is pushed out, making the cylinder ready for the next cycle. The fuel for most sports car engines is gasoline. The gasoline is turned into tiny droplets and mixed with air before it goes into the cylinder. The explosion is set off by a tiny spark made by a **spark plug.**

CYLINDERS AND VALVES

Each cylinder in an engine has holes in the top that let fuel and air in and let exhaust gases out. Each hole has a **valve** that opens and closes the hole. Rotating rods called cam shafts make the valves open and close.

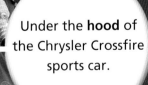

Under the **hood** of the Chrysler Crossfire sports car.

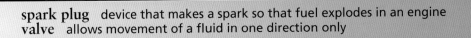

spark plug   device that makes a spark so that fuel explodes in an engine
valve   allows movement of a fluid in one direction only

ENGINE STATISTICS

The **capacity** of an engine is the space inside its **cylinders.** The bigger the capacity of an engine, the more powerful it is. Capacity is measured in liters or cubic centimeters (cc). Normal family cars have engines with capacities from about 1 liter (1,000 cc) to about 2 liters (2,000 cc). Many sports car engines have capacities of more than 3 liters (3,000 cc). Some engines are as big as 6 liters (6,000 cc). An engine's power is measured in **horsepower (hp).** A normal car engine produces between 50 and 120 hp. Small sports car engines produce more than 150 hp. Big ones produce more than 500 hp.

PORSCHE V10

This engine powers the Porsche *Carrera GT*
- Type: V10
- Capacity: 5.7 liters
- Maximum revs: over 8,000 rpm
- **Valves**: four per cylinder
- Power: 603 hp
- **Transmission**: six-speed manual

capacity   total space inside all the cylinders in a car engine
cylinder   tube-shaped part of an engine where fuel is burned

V6

Flat 12

Straight 4

ENGINE ARRANGEMENTS

Normal car engines have only four cylinders. They are arranged in a straight line. This is called a straight-four engine. Sports car engines have six, eight, ten, or even twelve cylinders. In these engines, the cylinders are in two rows. Half the cylinders are on one side of the engine and half on the other side. The cylinders are tilted outward to make a V shape. This kind of engine is called a V6, a V8, a V10, or a V12. In a few engines, the two rows of cylinders are on their sides, opposite each other. This is called a flat engine.

HIGH REVS

Each time a **piston** does its power stroke, it produces power for the car's wheels. The more often pistons do power strokes, the more power an engine produces. Normal car engines can rev up to about 6,000 rpm. Sports engines can rev up to about 8,000 rpm. A normal engine would break apart at this rate!

The BMW Z4 has a 3-liter, straight-6 engine arrangement.

3 4 5 6
2 7
1 8
0 9
x1000

horsepower (hp)   measurement of engine power
piston   sits inside the cylinder moving backward and forward

SUPERCHARGED

In most car engines, the **pistons** suck air and fuel into the **cylinders** on the intake stroke. Sports-car engines often have **superchargers** or **turbochargers**. These are pumps that force air and fuel into the cylinders. This lets the engine burn more fuel on each stroke, so it is more powerful. A supercharger pump is worked by the engine. A turbocharger pump is worked by the **exhaust** gases flowing out of the engine.

EXHAUSTS AND SILENCERS

High **capacity**, high-revving sports car engines produce lots of exhaust gases. They often have twin exhausts, with twin catalytic converters. These take poisonous gases out of the exhaust gases. Silencer boxes reduce the noise of the exhaust gases roaring from the engine.

TRACTION CONTROL

Because a sports car has such a powerful engine, it is easy to do a wheel spin by accident. An electronic system called traction control senses if the wheels are spinning. Then, it automatically reduces the engine revs until the tires grip again.

The twin exhaust pipes at the rear of a TVR T440R.

clutch   device that is used to change gears
exhaust   waste gas from an engine

TRANSMISSIONS

A car's **transmission** connects its engine to its wheels. The transmission's **gears** allow the engine to turn the wheels at different speeds. Low gears are for starting off and high gears for high-speed driving. Transmissions can be manual, automatic, and semiautomatic. In a manual transmission, the driver changes gear with a stick shift and a **clutch** pedal. An automatic transmission changes gear by itself as the car speeds up and slows down.

TOYOTA SUPRA

- Date production started: 1993
- Where made: Japan
- **Chassis: unitary**
- Engine position: front
- Engine type: 3.0-liter twin turbo straight-6
- Power: 326 **hp**
- **Acceleration**: 0–60 mph (96 km/h) in 5.1 seconds
- Top speed: 155 mph (249 km/h)

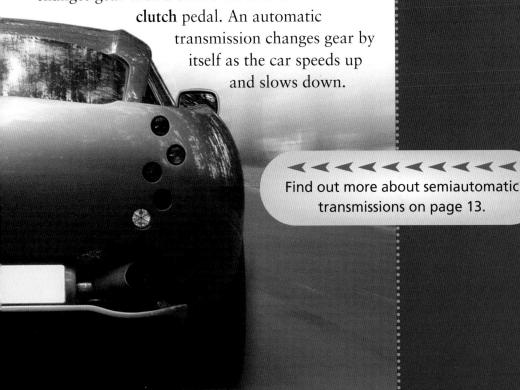

◄◄◄◄◄◄◄◄◄◄◄

Find out more about semiautomatic transmissions on page 13.

supercharger   device that blows air into an engine, driven by the engine
turbocharger   device that blows air into an engine, driven by exhaust gases

WHEELS

Sports cars have special wheels to increase their **performance. Alloy wheels** are made from lightweight metals. They are lighter than the solid steel wheels on ordinary cars. Tires are the only parts of a car that touch the road. Sports cars need to grip the road well for performance and safety. Grip comes from the **friction** between the tires and the road surface. Sports cars tires are wider than ordinary tires. Wide tires have more rubber in contact with the road, giving the extra grip that sports cars need. Grooves in the tires, called tread, squeeze water from under the tires.

SUSPENSIONS

Sports cars have stiff **suspensions** to stop them from rolling from side to side on bumpy roads and sharp bends. Many sports cars have a special suspension called a double wishbone suspension. It keeps the tires flat on the road all the time.

air duct   one of the holes in a car body that funnels air to cool the brakes

An alloy sports car wheel fitted with a sports tire.

SPEEDING UP

As a sports car speeds up, the wide tires push back on the road. This pushes the car forward. As the car brakes, the wide tires push forward on the road, slowing it quickly. As the car zips around a corner, the tires push sideways, stopping the car from sliding.

SLOWING DOWN

Sports cars need strong brakes for slowing quickly from high speed. Each wheel has a disc attached to it. When the driver presses the brake pedal, brake pads press hard on the discs. Friction between the pads and discs slows the car. Bigger sports cars often have two sets of pads on each disc for extra stopping power.

COOLING BRAKES

Friction between brake pads and discs makes lots of heat. Sports car brakes can get very hot. The discs and pads are made from special materials that do not melt. **Air ducts** make air flow over the brakes, helping to cool them.

---

friction   force that tries to stop surfaces from sliding past each other
suspension   system in a car that absorbs bumps in the road surface

SUPERCARS

Some sports cars are very special. They have amazing **acceleration** and top speeds. These are the **supercars.** They are the kings of the sports car world. They also have incredible prices. They are so expensive that only top sports stars, rock stars, and extremely wealthy people can afford to buy them.

PRODUCTION

Ordinary family cars and many sports cars are built by mass production. This means that thousands of each model of car are made in huge factories. Supercar **manufacturers** make only a few hundred of their supercars. They are normally built one by one by craftspeople.

PEAK PERFORMANCE

Supercars are the ultimate road-going cars. Top supercars accelerate as quickly as **Formula One** racing cars and easily match their top speeds. From a standing start, a supercar reaches 60 mph (96 km/h) in about four seconds. A few seconds later it can be traveling at more than 200 mph (320 km/h). For **performance** like this, a supercar needs an engine that produces more than 500 **hp.** The car needs to be made of lightweight materials.

Formula One   type of racing for specially made cars that is especially popular in Europe

SUPERCAR BUILDERS

Supercars are normally designed to be driven on the road. Special versions of them are built for the race track. Other supercars are road-going versions of racing cars. Supercar manufacturers like to hold the title of world's fastest **production car.** In 2003 this was held by the McLaren *F1*, at 240 mph (386 km/h). Famous supercar makers include Jaguar, Ferrari, and Lamborghini.

MERCEDES McLAREN SLR

- Date production started: 2004
- Where made: Germany
- **Chassis: carbon-fiber monocoque**
- Engine position: front
- Engine type: 5.5 liter **supercharged** V8
- Power: 626 hp
- Acceleration: 0–60 mph (96 km/h) in 3.8 seconds
- Top speed: 208 mph (335 km/h)

The body panels and doors of the Mercedes *SLR* are made from lightweight **aluminum.**

production car   car built in large numbers for general sale
supercar   sports car with incredible performance

RACING TECHNOLOGY

The **engineers** who design racing cars are always developing new ways to make their cars faster, easier to drive, and safer. **Supercar** makers often build racing cars, too. They use **technology** from their racing cars in their supercars. Some supercars are really racing cars with changes to make them "street legal." They have a lightweight racing-car **chassis,** high-power racing engines, and racing-car controls.

McLAREN F1

The McLaren *F1* was the world's fastest **production car** for more than ten years. It costs almost one million dollars to buy one. The *F1* was based on McLaren's successful Formula One racing car.

McLAREN F1

- Date production started: 1993
- Where made: United Kingdom
- Chassis: carbon-fiber monocoque
- Engine position: mid-engined
- Engine type: 6.0-liter V12
- Power: 627 **hp**
- **Acceleration**: 0–60 mph (96 km/h) in 3.2 seconds
- Top speed: 240 mph (386 km/h)

adjust   change to fit new needs
engineer   person who uses science to design and build cars

FORMULA ONE ROAD CAR

The Ferrari *F50* supercar was designed and built to celebrate the fiftieth birthday of the Ferrari company. The car was based on Ferrari's **Formula One** racing car used in the 1990 season. Underneath the bright red body is a super-strong, **carbon-fiber, monocoque** chassis. Bolted to the back of the monocoque is a 4.7-liter V12 engine. It is a bigger version of the engine from the racing car. The *F50* has electronically controlled **suspension** that **adjusts** to how rough the road is.

The *F50* is not a **luxury** supercar. The engine is very noisy and the inside is rather bare. But this makes drivers feel they are sitting in a road-going racer!

Q&A

Q: How many Ferrari *F50* cars were built?

A: Only 349.

The Ferrari *F50's* body was designed by Pininfarina.

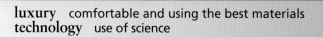

F50 CON

luxury comfortable and using the best materials
technology use of science

CLASSIC SPORTS CARS

The very first motor car was built by German **engineer** Karl Benz in 1885. It looked like a horse-drawn carriage with an engine bolted onto the back. In fact, that is exactly what it was! Engine power was just one **horsepower.** Top speed was just 9 mph (14 km/h). Benz's car was an amazing machine at the time, but it was hardly a sports car. Motor engineers quickly designed more powerful engines, giving cars better top speeds. Soon drivers became interested in going fast. They also started racing against one another.

EARLY AERODYNAMICS

In the 1920s racing-car makers began designing **aerodynamic** bodies to make their cars faster. Sports car **manufacturers** copied the idea. They designed the first **coupes.** This style of car became known as the **grand tourer,** or **GT.**

◄◄◄◄◄◄◄◄◄◄◄

Find out more about the GT on page 10.

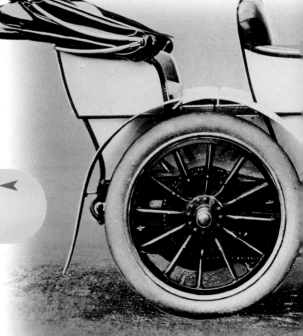

coupe   sports car with a body that curves gently from the roof to the rear

THE FIRST SPORTS CAR

Most car historians think that the first sports car was the Mercedes *35 hp*. This car was built in 1901 by the Daimler company in Germany. The "35 hp" part of the name stood for 35 horsepower. This was the power of the engine. The car was named Mercedes after the daughter of one of Daimler's salesmen. The Mercedes *35 hp* had many new technical ideas, including a lightweight **chassis** and mechanical engine **valves.** It was faster than other cars of the time and won many races. Top speed was more than 60 mph (96 km/h).

<<<<<<<<<<

Find out how a supercharger works on page 24.

SUPERCHARGERS

A **supercharger** makes an engine more powerful. The supercharger was invented in the 1920s for racing cars. It soon appeared on road-going cars, too. This Bugatti *type 55* was one of the first road cars to have a supercharger.

The Mercedes *35-hp* was designed by the famous German **engineer** Wilhelm Maybach.

grand tourer (GT)   another name for a coupe

33

FASTER AND FASTER

Dozens of companies in Europe and the United States were building sports cars when World War II began in 1939. By then, the best sports cars could manage top speeds of more than 100 mph (160 km/h).

FIRST TO 120 MPH

The Jaguar *XK120* was shown to the public for the first time at the 1948 London Motor Show. The "120" part of its name stood for 120 mph (193 km/h). The *XK120* was the first **production car** that could reach that speed. The engine was so good that it was still being put into new Jaguars in the 1990s. The *XK120* was very popular in the United States, where there were few sports cars at first.

A Jaguar *XK120* taking part in a race in the 1950s.

ITALIAN AND U.S. FIRSTS

One of Ferrari's first sports cars was also built in 1948. It was the Ferrari *166 Inter,* designed by Enzo Ferrari. Ferrari only made the **chassis** and engine. Customers had to buy their own car bodies. Top speed for the *166* was 105 mph (169 km/h). Until the 1950s, most sports cars bought by Americans were made in Europe. Then, the American **manufacturer** General Motors designed the Chevrolet *Corvette.* The original straight-6 engine was replaced by a more powerful V8, which improved its top speed to 120 mph (193 km/h).

007'S ASTON MARTIN

Aston Martin is a famous British sports car maker. Its Aston Martin *DB5* **coupe** (pictured above) was made famous in 1964 by the James Bond movie *Goldfinger.* Bond's *DB5* also had machine guns and an ejector seat.

CHEVROLET CORVETTE

- Date production started: 1953
- Where made: United States
- Chassis: box section
- Engine position: front
- Engine type: 3.8-liter straight-6
- Power: 150 **hp**
- **Acceleration:** 0–60 mph (96 km/h) in 11.2 seconds
- Top speed: 105 mph (169 km/h)

AGE OF THE SUPERCARS

In the 1960s a new type of sports car appeared on the roads. It was the **supercar**. These extraordinary cars featured a mixture of enormous power, beautiful design, and huge price tags. The Italian company Lamborghini was one of the first supercar **manufacturers.** Its first car was built in 1966. It was called the *Miura*. It had a top speed of 171 mph (275 km/h). A few years later Lamborghini replaced the *Miura* with a new model, the *Countach*. Its 3.9-liter V12 engine gave it a top speed of 175 mph (282 km/h). Both cars were mid-engined.

LAMBORGHINI COUNTACH

- Date production started: 1971
- Where made: Italy
- **Chassis:** tubular steel
- Engine position: mid-engined
- Engine type: 3.9-liter V12
- **Power:** 375 **hp**
- **Acceleration:** 0–60 mph (96 km/h) in 5.7 seconds
- Top speed: 175 mph (282 km/h)

manufacturer   company that designs and builds cars

OLD AND NEW STYLES

Most modern sports cars have a **sleek** look. They have smooth, rounded, **aerodynamic** bodies. They are definitely machines of the 21st century. But many sports-car **enthusiasts** love the look of the two-seater sports cars of the 1920s and 1930s. Real classic cars are hard to find and expensive to buy and repair. So a few manufacturers build new sports cars in the old style. They have narrow bodies, arches over the wheels, and small windshields. Some examples are the Morgan 8 and the Caterham 7, both made in the United Kingdom. These cars might look old, but underneath they are modern sports machines.

The Morgan *Aero 8:* A classic style with modern **technology.**

ROAD RUNNER

The extraordinary Plymouth *Road Runner Superbird* was named after the Road Runner cartoon character. It was designed for the road and for racing in **NASCAR** races. On the track it could reach 190 mph (306 km/h).

RACING SPORTS CARS

When you think of a racing car, you probably think of a specially built racer such as a **Formula One** car or an **Indy Car**. But most motor races are between sports cars like the ones you see on the public roads.

LACK OF LUXURY

Racing sports cars are not built for comfort! The car is stripped of all its **luxury** fittings for the race track. It makes the car lighter. Only the most important controls and instruments are left.

RACING MODIFICATIONS

Sports cars designed for the public roads are **modified** for the track. The modifications improve the car's **performance,** allowing it to speed up faster, brake more quickly, and corner faster. Wings and skirts are **aerodynamic** modifications. They help to press the car onto the road for better grip on corners. Racing tires made from soft rubber also make the car grip better. Stronger brakes allow drivers to brake later as they approach corners.

The racing version of the Peugeot *307* with **spoiler** and **alloy wheels.**

Indy Car   type of racing car that is the American version of a Formula One car

ENGINE TUNING

Racing cars have more powerful engines than road-going sports cars. Sometimes the engine has a bigger **capacity.** It is also race **tuned,** which means it **adjusts** to get the most power possible from the engine. The **valve** timings are adjusted so that the engine's valves open and close at exactly the right time for fuel and air to get into the cylinders and for **exhaust** gases to get out. The air inlets and exhausts are bigger. This lets more fuel in and more exhaust gases out.

MERCEDES BENZ CLK-GTR

- Date production started: 1998
- Where made: Germany
- **Chassis: carbon-fiber monocoque**
- Engine position: mid-engined
- Engine type: 6.8-liter V12
- Power: 612 **hp**
- **Acceleration:** 0–60 mph (96 km/h) in 3.8 seconds
- Top speed: 199 mph (320 km/h)

The road-going **convertible** version of the Peugeot *307*.

modified   changed
tuned   adjusted to give maximum power

ONE-MODEL RACE

A one-model race is a race for just one model of sports car. These races are for sports car owners who want to try out their driving skills on the race track.

TRACK RACING

Most sports car races are held on race tracks. There are many different race-track competitions. Some competitions are single races for local drivers. The drivers own the cars and service them themselves. Some competitions are world championships that are made up of many races on different race tracks. The cars are built by sports car **manufacturers** and driven by professional drivers.

RACING CLASSES

Sports cars are divided into different classes for racing. This means that cars with similar **performance** race against each other. Some competitions are reserved for road-going sports cars and some are for cars that are built just for racing.

Drivers warm up their tires on a practice lap before the big race.

TOP RACES

The World **GT** Car Championship is for road-going sports cars. The Sportscar Championship is for specially built racing sports cars. In the United States, the top sports car championship is **NASCAR.** Years ago, NASCAR cars were **production cars modified** for the race track. Now, they are built just for racing.

A NASCAR pit stop. The team are changing tires and refueling.

RULES

Each competition has it own strict rules. Technical rules tell the **engineers** exactly what features the cars are allowed to have. For example, they say the maximum or minimum size of the car's body, the engine size, and tire sizes.

PRODUCTION CAR RULES

There is a special rule for production sports car racing. A certain number of each car model must be made for use on the road before that model can enter a race.

LE MANS TRIVIA

- The first Le Mans race was in 1923.

- Until 1969 the race began with the drivers running to their cars. Now they start sitting in their cars.

- Belgian driver Jacky Ickx won Le Mans six times between 1969 and 1982.

- In 1995 the McLaren *F1* was the first production car to win the race since the 1940s.

- In 2003 the winning Bentley car completed 377 laps.

- 250,000 people watch the race every year.

RACING AT LE MANS

The Le Mans 24-Hour Race is one of the world's most famous sports car races. It is not only a race, but also a tough test of strength for both cars and drivers. The car that travels farthest in 24 hours is the winner. The race is held every year near Le Mans in France.

THE COURSE

The Le Mans course is 8.5 miles (13.6 kilometers) long. It is made up of the Sarthe motor-racing circuit and some lengths of public roads.

The most famous part of the circuit is the Mulsanne straight, which is 3.5 miles (5.7 kilometers) long. By 1989 cars were whizzing down the straight at more than 250 mph (400 km/h). After that, **chicanes** were added to slow down the cars for safety.

LE MANS TYPES

Two types of cars can enter Le Mans. The first type is **GT** sports cars. These must be racing models of road-going **production cars,** such as the Porsche *911 GT* and the Ferrari *360 Modena*. The second type is **prototype** cars. These are specially built single-seater racing sports cars. They are built and raced by major **manufacturers** such as Audi and BMW. A prototype car almost always wins the race, because prototypes have better **performance** than road-going cars.

This is the road-going version of the Dodge *Viper GTS-R* that is raced at Le Mans.

DODGE VIPER GTS-R

- Date production started: 2000
- Where made: United States
- **Chassis:** tubular
- Engine position: front
- Engine type: 8-liter V10
- Power: 500 **hp**
- **Acceleration:** 0–60 mph (96 km/h) in 5.3 seconds
- Top speed: 172 mph (277 km/h)

prototype   first model used to test the success of a design

RALLY RACING

Sports cars also race in **rallies**. A rally is a long-distance race along public roads, rough tracks, and across country. Rally cars ride over **tarmac**, dusty gravel, mud, and ice at speeds of up to 125 mph (200 km/h). The top race in rallying is the World Rally Championship. Teams take part in fourteen rallies around the world. Each rally lasts for three days and is made up of about twenty sections, called stages. The cars drive over the stages one after the other. The times for each stage are added together, and the car with the quickest time wins.

codriver   in rallying, a person who gives the driver information about the road ahead

RALLY CAR FEATURES

Rally cars must be extremely tough to stay in one piece on the bumpy roads. World rally cars are **modified production cars**. But only the shape of the car is left!

A world rally car costs almost one million dollars to make. It has a super-strong **chassis** and a roll cage (a strong, protective cage) to protect the driver and **codriver**. Its 2-liter **turbocharged** engine produces 300 **hp**. The **gears** are semiautomatic and **adjust** up or down in less than a tenth of a second. After each stage, **mechanics** are allowed just twenty minutes to repair the cars.

The service area at the 2003 Rally of Catalonia, Spain.

SUBARU IMPREZA WRX

- Date production started: 1993
- Where made: Japan
- Chassis: **unitary**
- Engine position: front
- Engine type: 2-liter flat-4
- Power: 280 hp
- **Acceleration**: 0–60 mph (96 km/h) in 4.7 seconds
- Top speed: 150 mph (241 km/h)

DRIVING A SPORTS CAR

Driving a sports car at high speed is very different from driving an ordinary family car around town. A sports car driver needs quick reactions. This means he can recover from skids or swerves and overtake or avoid other cars. Races are often won by the driver who takes the track's corners at the highest speed possible. Slowing too much for a corner wastes time. But if a driver takes a corner too fast, the tires cannot grip the road, and the car spins off the track.

SAFETY FIRST

Even the best race drivers sometimes crash in their sports cars. But modern sports cars are very safe. They feature protective roll cages and seat belts. The driver also wears a crash helmet and fireproof overalls.

mechanic   person who knows how to repair and build cars

MAKING ADJUSTMENTS

Racing drivers also have to understand how their cars work. Cars often oversteer or understeer on corners. That means they turn too much or not enough. Drivers must understand why this happens. They ask the team's **mechanics** to **adjust** the car's wings and **suspension** to fix the problem.

RALLY DRIVERS

Rally drivers have to focus hard to drive on narrow, bumpy, slippery roads. The **codriver** tells the driver what bends, bumps, and other obstacles are coming up on the road.

THE RACING LINE

Drivers try to learn the fastest way around a race track before racing for real. They figure out where to start turning to take each corner and then what line to take through the corner. Drivers call this the racing line.

Rally cars often go into the air on humps and bumps.

MAKERS AND DESIGNERS

Motor **manufacturers** such as Ferrari, Audi, and Jaguar have become famous for their sports cars. People expect these cars to have great looks as well as a great **performance,** so it is important to have a good **stylist** to design the cars. A few sports car stylists have become as famous as the cars they designed.

A BUGATTI REVIVAL

Volkswagen took over the Bugatti name in 1998. They built a Bugatti **supercar** called the *Veyron* in 2004. It is the fastest **production car** ever.

BUGATTI

Bugatti is one of the most famous names in sports car history. Bugatti's best cars were made in the 1920s and 1930s. They won many races on the track, including Le Mans in the 1930s. The Bugatti company was started in 1910 by Italian motor designer Ettore Bugatti.

▶▶▶▶▶▶▶▶▶▶

Find out more about the *Veyron* on page 57.

radiator   part of a car that cools hot waste from the engine

Ettore Bugatti (standing, in hat) and Jean Bugatti (in car) in 1939.

BUGATTI'S CARS

Ettore Bugatti designed the *Type 35* Bugatti in 1924. Many **enthusiasts** think this two-seater is the most beautiful sports car ever made. Ettore's oldest son was Jean Bugatti. Jean was a great **engineer** and a talented stylist. He designed the sleek Bugatti cars of the 1930s, such as the *Type 57* **coupe.** Jean was killed in 1939 testing one of his own cars. Ettore died in 1947, and the company stopped making cars.

THE FAMOUS BUGATTI RADIATOR

Every sports car maker has its own symbol that appears on every car. Every Bugatti had a **radiator** shaped like an upside-down horseshoe (see blue Bugatti on page 48). At the top is a red badge with the famous Bugatti name.

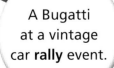

A Bugatti at a vintage car **rally** event.

stylist   person who designs the shape of a car

ITALIAN STYLE

Italy was the home of the greatest sports car **stylists.** They designed cars for famous **manufacturers** in Italy and in other countries, too. Pininfarina is a company that is famous for its car design. It was started by Giovan (pronounced "jo-van") Battista Farina (left). He had nine older brothers and was known as Pinin. That means "little boy" in Italian. Farina was born in 1895 and started his career at his brother's car-making company. He started Pininfarina in 1930. The company designed cars for Lancia and Fiat. Its most famous designs were for Ferrari, such as the Ferrari *Daytona*, Ferrari *F-40*, and Ferrari *Enzo*.

The *Dino* of the 1960s, one of Pininfarina's designs for Fiat.

GHIA

The word *Ghia* appears on many modern Ford cars. It means that the car has special extras such as **alloy wheels** and electric windows. Ghia was an Italian company named after designer Giacinto Ghia. It built sports car bodies for Alfa Romeo, Maserati, and Porsche.

GANDINI

Marcello Gandini was born in 1938. His first job was to repair damaged car bodies, but he went on to design them instead. In the 1960s he worked for the Bertone company. Here, he designed the Lamborghini *Miura*, one of the first **supercars.** This amazing car made him famous. Then, he designed sports cars for Ferrari, Maserati, Alfa Romeo, and Fiat. In 1971 he designed the spectacular Lamborghini *Countach*.

The flowing lines of Marcello Gandini's Lamborghini *Miura*.

FERRARI 550 BARCHETTA

- Date production started: 2000
- Where made: Italy
- **Chassis:** tubular
- Engine position: front
- Engine type: 5.5-liter V12
- Power: 485 **hp**
- **Acceleration:** 0–60 mph (96 km/h) in 4.4 seconds
- Top speed: 186 mph (299 km/h)

FERRARI

Ferrari is the most famous name in the history of sports cars. Almost every Ferrari model is a classic car. People who love sports cars dream of having their own Ferrari. A few lucky ones do. The man behind the company was Enzo Ferrari. He was born in Italy in 1898. When he was a boy, Enzo went to several motor races. He decided to become a racing driver. He turned out to be good at it, and Alfa Romeo gave him a job on their racing team. In the 1920s and 1930s Enzo built and raced cars for Alfa Romeo with great success.

Enzo Ferrari testing an Alfa Romeo racer in 1924.

FERRARI BIRTHDAYS

To celebrate its fortieth birthday in 1987, Ferrari built the *F40* **supercar.** Its top speed is 200 mph (322 km/h). Ten years later, it built the *F50* to celebrate its fiftieth birthday.

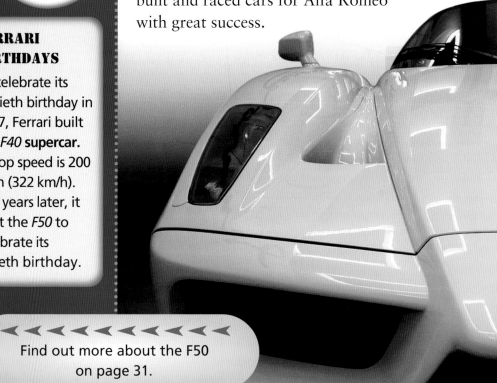

Find out more about the F50 on page 31.

FERRARIS ON THE ROAD

In 1943 Enzo set up a factory at Maranello in Italy. The company's first car was the Ferrari *125 Sport*. This was designed to be a racing car as well as a road car. Enzo was always most interested in racing. He said that he sold sports cars to pay for the company's racing teams. Famous Ferrari cars include the *Daytona*, the *Dino*, and the *Testarossa*. Enzo's favorite was the *250 GTO*. Enzo Ferrari died in 1988. The Ferrari *Enzo* (below), launched in 2002, is named after him.

The *Enzo* is the same *F1* car driven by top racer Michael Schumacher, but with a body on top.

THE PRANCING HORSE

In 1923 Enzo Ferrari met the parents of Francesco Baracca, a famous Italian World War I pilot. They gave him a badge from their son's squadron (fighting unit). It was the prancing horse that became Ferrari's badge.

PORSCHE

Porsche is one of Germany's leading sports car companies. It is successful on the road and on the track. The company is named after Dr. Ferdinand Porsche. He was born in 1875. He quickly became famous as an **engineer** and test driver. He then worked for the German car maker Daimler. In the 1930s Ferdinand Porsche designed the first Volkswagen. This car later became known as the famous Beetle. The first Porsche sports car was made in 1948. It was based on the Volkswagen and was called the *Porsche 356*. It featured a rear engine and could do 85 mph (137 km/h).

A **convertible** version of the Volkswagen, pictured in 1938.

An early Porsche *911*. This is the **coupe** version.

THE PORSCHE 911

At the 1963 Frankfurt Motor Show, Porsche showed off its new sports car. It was the Porsche *911*, one of the greatest sports cars ever. Like the *356*, the *911* has a rear engine. But the engine is more powerful, with six **cylinders.** The body was designed by Ferdinand Porsche's son.

A **turbocharged** version of the *911* was developed in 1974. There have been many versions of the Porsche *911* since 1963. The shape has gradually changed, but the *911* is still being made.

PORSCHE 911 GT2

- Date production started: 2001
- Where made: Germany
- **Chassis: unitary**
- Engine position: rear
- Engine type: 3.6-liter turbocharged flat-6
- Power: 462 **hp**
- **Acceleration:** 0–60 mph (96 km/h) in 4.1 seconds
- Top speed: 196 mph (315 km/h)

DESIGNING A SUPERCAR

TESTING AND PRODUCTION

Testing is an important part of making a new car. Engineers make and test every part of the new supercar. They make a **prototype** car to drive to make sure it is safe. They also do **aerodynamic** tests in a wind tunnel.

Sports car **manufacturers** build **supercars** to help sell their other sports cars and to make sure they have good racing teams. They want people to like their supercars, since it makes people talk about them. A supercar also shows off a company's new **technology.** Some supercars are made to celebrate important dates in a company's history.

SKETCHY START

Supercars start life as ideas in the heads of company bosses. Then, a team of people start work to make the car a reality. A **stylist** takes the ideas and makes lots of rough sketches on paper. After many discussions and new sketches, the stylist figures out a final look for the car.

The *Bengal*, a concept car displayed by Buick in 2003.

DESIGNING THE CAR

The stylist designs the seats, dashboard, and instruments as well as the body. **Engineers** figure out which materials to use for the **chassis** and body. Engineers also decide what engine will power the car and choose a **transmission** and wheels.

Designer working on a mock-up of a Chrysler *Crossfire*.

CONCEPT CARS

Finally, the first car is built. Now it is time for the public to see the new supercar. It is displayed in Detroit, Paris, or Tokyo at the top car shows. There is no guarantee that it will be a **production car.** At the moment it is called a concept car. If the public likes it, a new supercar may go into production. You could be seeing one on the road very soon.

BUGATTI VEYRON

- Date production started: 2004
- Where made: Italy
- Chassis: **unitary**
- Engine position: mid-engined
- Engine type: 8.0-liter twin V8
- Power: 987 **hp**
- **Acceleration**: 0–60 mph (96 km/h) in 3.0 seconds
- Top speed: 252 mph (406 km/h)

SPORTS CAR FACTS

WORLD RALLY CHAMPIONS

Year	Driver	Manufacturer
2003	Petter Solberg	Subaru
2002	Marcus Gronhölm	Peugeot
2001	Richard Burns	Subaru
2000	Marcus Gronhölm	Peugeot
1999	Tommi Makinen	Mitsubishi
1998	Tommi Makinen	Mitsubishi

LE MANS WINNERS

Year	Car	Winners
2003	Bentley Exp Speed 8	Tom Kristensen, Guy Smith, Dindo Capello
2002	Audi R8	Frank Biela, Tom Kristensen, Emanuele Pirro
2001	Audi R8	Frank Biela, Tom Kristensen, Emanuele Pirro
2000	Audi R8	Frank Biela, Tom Kristensen, Emanuele Pirro
1999	BMW V12 LMR	Pierluigi Martini, Yannick Dalmas, Joachim Winkelhock
1998	Porsche 911 GT1-98	Allan McNish, Laurent Aiello, Stephane Ortelli

SPORTS CAR ON WATER

The Aquada Sports Amphibian is a sports car that turns into a sports boat at the touch of a button. It has a top speed of 100 mph (160 km/h) on land and 30 mph (48 km/h) on water.

FASTEST SUPERCARS

Car	0–60 mph	Year
Bugatti Veyron	3.0 secs	2004
McLaren F1	3.2 secs	1993
Ferrari Enzo	3.6 secs	2002
Pagani Zonda	3.7 secs	2002
Mercedes Benz CLK-GTR	3.8 secs	1998
Dodge Viper	3.9 secs	2003
Noble M12 GTO	3.9 secs	2000
Jaguar XJ220	4.0 secs	1993
Porsche 911 Turbo	4.2 secs	2000
Ferrari Modena	4.3 secs	2000
TVR Tuscan	4.3 secs	2001
Aston Martin Vanquish	4.7 secs	2000
Lotus Elise 111R	4.9 secs	2004
Morgan Aero 8	4.9 secs	2000
Toyota Supra Turbo	5.3 secs	1998
BMW Z4	5.4 secs	2003
Lamborghini Countach	5.6 secs	1982
Mazda RX-8	6.4 secs	2003
Lamborghini Miura	6.7 secs	1971

DAKAR RALLY WINNERS (CAR CATEGORY)

Year	Drivers	Manufacturer
2004	Stephane Peterhansel, Jean-Paul Cottret	Mitsubishi
2003	Hiroshi Masuoka, Andreas Schulz	Mitsubishi
2002	Hiroshi Masuoka, Pascal Maimon	Mitsubishi
2001	Jutta Kleinschmidt, Andreas Schulz	Mitsubishi
2000	Jean-Louis Schlesser, Henri Magne	Renault
1999	Jean-Louis Schlesser, Henri Magne	Renault
1998	Jean-Pierre Fontenay, Gilles Picard	Mitsubishi

FIND OUT MORE

ORGANIZATIONS

**Grand American
Road Racing
Association**
1801 West
International
Speedway Blvd.
Daytona Beach, FL
32114-1243
webmaster@
grandamerican.com

**International Motor
Sports Association**
1394 Broadway Ave.
Braselton, Georgia
30517
info@imsaracing.net

NASCAR
P.O. Box 2875
Daytona Beach, FL
32120
fanfeedback@nascar
.com

BOOKS

Graham, Ian. *Designed for Success: Sports Cars.* Chicago: Heinemann Library, 2003.

Johnstone, Michael. *NASCAR.* Minneapolis, Minn.: Lerner Publishing, 2003.

Lord, Trevor. *Big Book of Race Cars.* New York: Dorling Kindersley, 2001.

Maynard, Christopher. *Supreme Machines: Racing Cars.* Hauppauge, N.Y.: Barron's Educational Series, 1999.

Pitt, Matthew. *Formula One.* Danbury, Conn.: Scholastic Library, 2001.

WORLD WIDE WEB

If you want to find out more about sports cars, you can search the Internet using keywords like these:
Aston Martin cars
Enzo Ferrari
Lamborghini cars
Jaguar sport cars
Jean Bugatti
Porsche cars
supercars
World **Rally**
NASCAR
monocoque chassis
V12 engine

Make your own keywords using headings or words from this book. The search tips on the next page will help you to find the most useful websites.

SEARCH TIPS

There are billions of pages on the Internet, so it can be difficult to find exactly what you want to find. If you just type in "car" on a search engine such as Google, you will get a list of millions of web pages. These search skills will help you find useful websites more quickly.

- Use simple keywords, not whole sentences.
- Use two to six keywords in a search.
- Be precise—only use names of people, places, or things.
- If you want to find words that go together, put quote marks around them—for example "world speed record."
- Use the advanced section of your search engine.
- Use the "+" sign between keywords to find pages with all these words.

WHERE TO SEARCH

SEARCH ENGINE

Each search engine looks through millions of web pages and lists all sites that match the search words. The best matches are at the top of the list, on the first page. Try **google.com**.

SEARCH DIRECTORY

A search directory is like a library of websites. You can try searching by keyword or subject and browse through the different sites as you would look through books on a library shelf. A good example is **yahooligans.com**.

GLOSSARY

accelerate speed up

acceleration how quickly a car speeds up

accelerator foot pedal used to make a car's engine produce more or less power

adjust change to fit new needs

aerodynamics science of how air flows around moving objects

air duct one of the holes in a car body that funnels air to cool the brakes

alloy wheels wheels made from lightweight alloy metal

aluminum strong, lightweight metal

capacity total space inside all the cylinders of a car engine

carbon fiber very hard, strong, light material

chassis framework that supports a car's body

chicane narrow part of a race track that makes cars slow down

clutch device that is used to change gears

codriver in rallying, a person who gives the driver information about the road ahead

cooling duct one of the pipes that carries air to an engine to cool it

convertible car with a roof that can be removed

coupe sports car with a body that curves gently from the roof to the rear

crankshaft part of an engine that turns and is connected to the transmission

cylinder tube-shaped part of an engine where fuel is burned

deflector device that makes air hitting a car flow to one side

drag force that tries to stop things from moving through the air

drop-top car with a fold-down roof

engineer person who uses science to design and build cars

enthusiast person who really enjoys a particular hobby

exhaust waste gas from an engine

four-wheel drive vehicle with all four wheels turned by the engine

Formula One type of racing for specially made cars that is especially popular in Europe

friction force that tries to stop surfaces from sliding past each other

front-wheel drive vehicle with front wheels turned directly by the engine

gear one of two or more levels in a car that control its direction and speed

grand tourer (GT) another name for a coupe

handling car's ability to go around corners quickly without losing control

hood   movable metal cover over the front of a car

horsepower (hp)   measurement of engine power

Indy Car   type of racing car that is the American version of a Formula One car

internal combustion   what happens when fuel burns inside an engine

kevlar   very strong type of fiber

luxury   comfortable and using the best materials

manufacturer   company that designs and builds cars

mechanic   person who knows how to repair and build cars

modified   changed

monocoque   single-piece chassis

NASCAR   National Association for Stock Car Auto Racing

performance   measure of a car's acceleration and top speed

piston   sits inside the cylinder and moves backward and forward

production car   car built in large numbers for general sale

prototype   first model used to test the success of a design

radiator   part of a car that cools hot waste from the engine

rally   cross-country race

rear-wheel drive   vehicle with rear wheels turned directly by the engine

rev counter   instrument that shows how quickly the engine's crankshaft is turning

revolution   one complete turn

roadster   two-seater sports car with no roof

sleek   smooth, with graceful lines

spark plug   device that makes a spark so that fuel explodes in an engine

speedometer   instrument that shows a car's speed

spoiler   piece like a shelf at the rear of a car that reduces drag

stylist   person who designs the shape of a car

supercar   sports car with incredible performance

supercharger   device that blows air into an engine, driven by the engine

suspension   system in a car that absorbs bumps in the road surface

tarmac   hard, smooth road covering

technology   use of science

transmission   machinery that connects a car's engine to its wheels

tuned   adjusted to give maximum power

turbocharger   device that blows air into an engine, driven by exhaust gases

unitary chassis   framework that includes a car's side and roof panels, floor, and engine compartment

valve   allows movement of a fluid in one direction only

INDEX